Let's Mak

Contents	Page

written by Pam Holden
photographs by Claire Watkins

Look at this volcano!
A volcano is a mountain
that blows up!

Hot rock, called lava, comes out of the top.
It runs down the mountain.

It's fun to make your own
volcano with lava coming out.

You can find all the things you need in the kitchen.

Get a bottle made of plastic,
a jug, and some vinegar.
Find some washing-up liquid
and red food dye.

You need baking soda, too.
Take everything outside.

First, put four big spoons of baking soda into the bottle.

Then you can use wet sand to make a big mountain around the bottle.

Now mix half a cup of water and half a cup of vinegar in the jug.

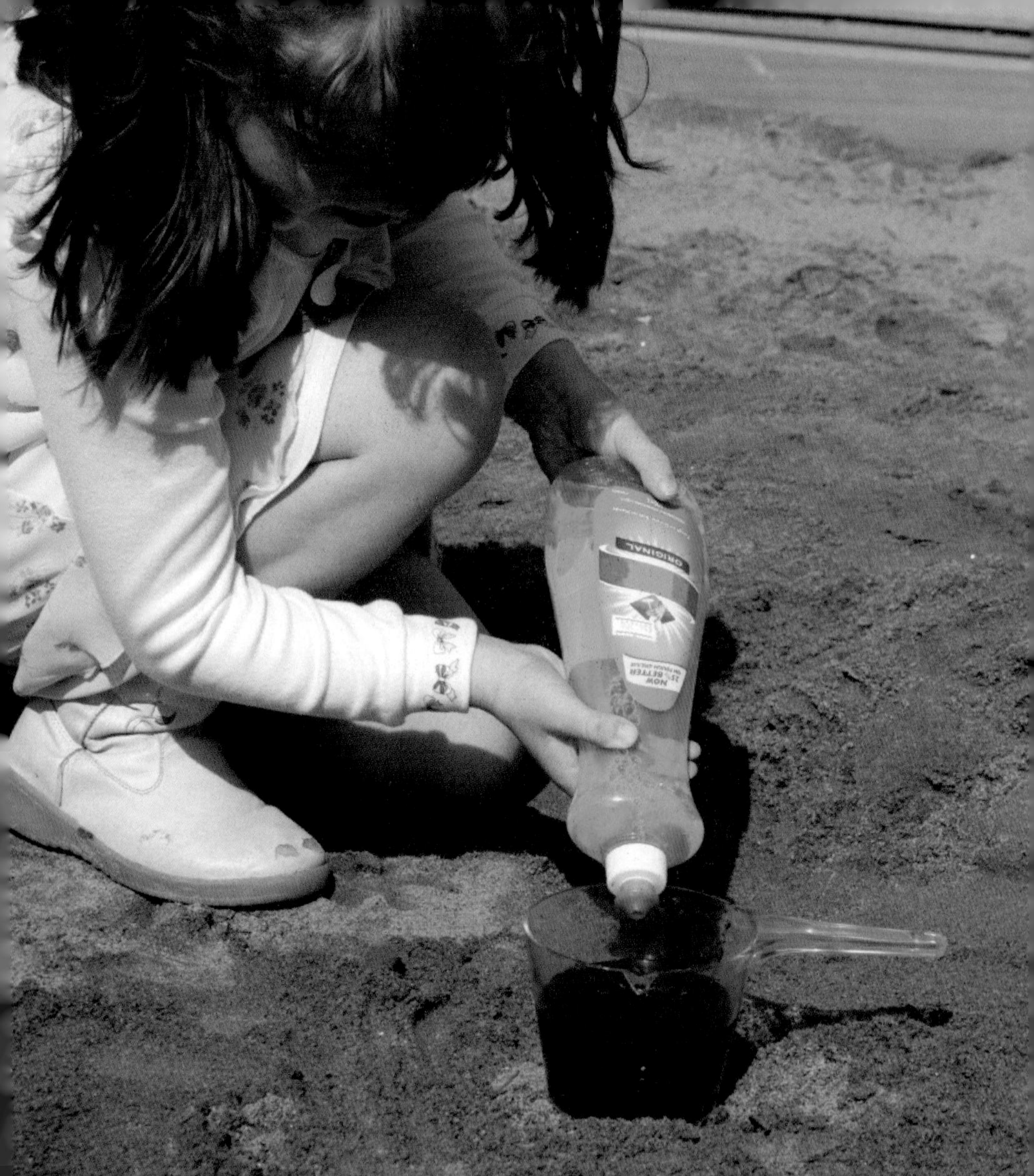

Next, put three drops of the washing-up liquid into the jug.

Then add two drops of red food dye.

Now pour the water and vinegar into the bottle in the sand.

Keep back! Lava will run down the mountain.